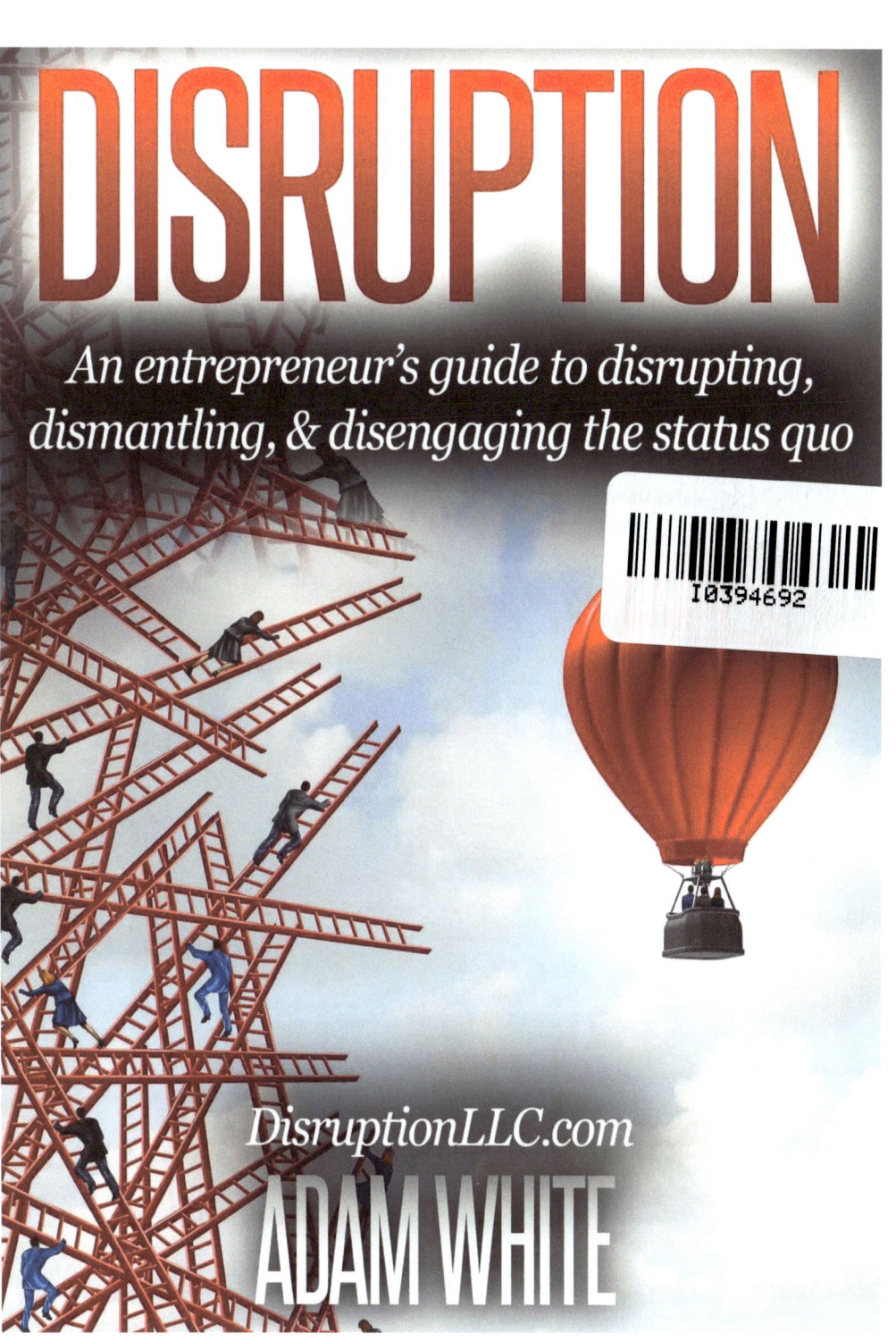

# DISRUPTION
# An Entrepreneurs Guide to Disrupting, Dismantling, & Disengaging From The Status Quo.

*by Adam White*

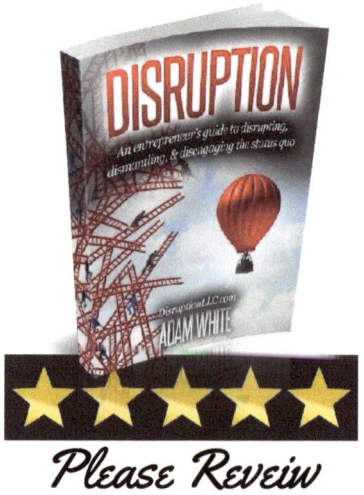

*Please Reveiw*

*disruptionllc.com*

**TURNKEY EBOOKS**

Fostering
Entrepreneurship
&
Effecting Change
Through Growth

TURNKEY EBOOKS

# Fortune favors the prepared mind.

## Louis Pasteur

*disruptionllc.com*

**TURNKEY EBOOKS**

## Table of Contents

Introduction .................................................................. 6

Nikola Tesla ................................................................ 21

Steve Jobs .................................................................. 22

Gary Vaynerchuck ...................................................... 24

Aaron Ross ................................................................ 26

Mark Zuckerberg ........................................................ 27

Michael Reynolds ....................................................... 29

Manoj Bhargava ......................................................... 31

Elon Musk .................................................................. 33

References ................................................................ 36

dis·rup·tion /disˈrəpSH(ə)n/
n. disturbance or problems that interrupt an event, activity, or process.

## Introduction

Disruption occurs when an event, often unexpected, interrupts the normal, course of events or challenges the unity of something. In the context of business, the term has come to refer to a new offering, a new business model or a new value proposition that challenges the dominance of an incumbent leader in a particular arena and has the potential to lead to its demise (Adler, 2015). Disrupting the market is primarily accomplished through establishing new business models, dismantling occurs through executing your new business model, and disengaging could be the act of turning your business model over to a CEO that is better equipped to sustain growth than a business founder. This eBook will give you an understanding of the term disruption as it pertains to the business market and introduce you to a few entrepreneurs who have totally smashed the status quo of things.

**TURNKEY EBOOKS**

The term "disruptive technology" as coined by Christensen (1997) refers to a new technology having lower cost and performance measured by traditional criteria, but having higher ancillary performance. In Christensen's theory of disruptive technology the establishment of a new market segment acts to channel the new product to the leading edge of the market or the early adopters. Once the innovation reaches the early to late majority of users it begins to compete with the established product in its traditional market (Utterback & Acee, 2003).

Christensen, in his book The Innovator's Dilemma, stated that there are two types of disruption:
1. New-market disruption- is where a new product meets the needs of a
market that was not previously being served.
2. Low-end disruption- In low end disruption, a startup offers a less expensive
and more convenient alternative to what previously existed.

**TURNKEY EBOOKS**

The phenomenon of digital disruption is certainly not a new one, however, the opportunities and risks it presents change and overtime and those who make the first move, history remembers as innovators (Nathan, 2016).

These are uncertain and challenging times for traditional organizations across every industry. The digital economy is turning the traditional rules of the game upside down, as a scan of business press headlines illustrates.

**TURNKEY EBOOKS**

This small sample of recent press headlines reveals why the leaders of traditional organizations might feel a strong sense of disquiet. Disruption can happen at any time, in any sector, and its effect on traditional organizations can be fundamental. Philippe Lemoine, who recently authored a report for the French government on the digital transformation of the country's economy, outlines three factors driving disruption: automation, dematerialization (substitution of physical products and processes with digital alternatives) and changes to the value chain. Disruptive technologies bring to a market a very different value proposition than had been available previously. Generally, disruptive technologies underperform established products in mainstream markets. But they have other features that a few fringe (and generally new) customers value. Products based on disruptive technologies are typically cheaper, simpler, smaller, and, frequently, more convenient to use (Christensen, 1997).

TURNKEY EBOOKS

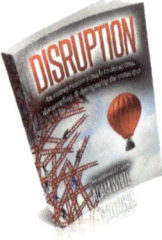

## Just consider

| | |
|---|---|
| Digital currencies | Social networks |
| | Immersive media. |
| The cloud | Augmented reality |
| | Big data analytics |
| 3D printing | Natural language processing |
| | Cognitive computing |
| Wearables | Quantum computing |
| | Drones |
| | Robots |
| MOOCs | Self-driving cars |
| E-books | Crowdsourcing |
| | Smart phones |
| E-commerce | Smart cities |
| | Enchanted objects |
| E-health | **The Internet** |
| Wireless broadband | **of Everything** |

**TURNKEY EBOOKS**

The list of potentially disruptive technologies keeps getting longer. Each one, by itself, is likely to have a substantial impact on many different aspects of society. Taken together, they are creating an environment that is dramatically different and far more volatile than the world that came before—an environment filled with novel challenges and opportunities (Adler, 2014). A notable characteristic of this period is the accelerating rate at which novel technologies keep appearing and evolving. We are witnessing the results of what Google Chief Economist Hal Varian has called "combinatorial innovation," that is the ready availability of component parts (each of which is evolving) that can be assembled in different ways to create new products and services. Virtually all of these technologies are digitally-based: they exist either as software or as combinations of hardware and software that take advantage of powerful, widely available, lowcost resources like the cloud and open source development tools. They leverage the power of digital computing and the global reach of the Internet to accelerate their development and speed their adoption (Adler, 2015).

*disruptionllc.com*

**TURNKEY EBOOKS**

In addition, the traditional development cycle has been compressed through a process of "lightweight innovation." Instead of spending long periods of time to create, test and refine a product, the new approach involves fast prototyping, quick release, then a continuous iterative process of product improvement based on user feedback that leads to scale and builds reliability. The first version of Gmail was written in one day, and the prototype of Twitter was developed in two weeks. (The first commercial version of Twitter was launched in 2006; a year later, it was generating 4 million tweets per day; by 2013, more than 200 million users were sending over 400 million tweets daily) (Adler, 2015).

*disruptionllc.com*

**TURNKEY EBOOKS**

Causing disruption is all about figuring out a way to be the only one who does what you do is a provocative goal, but it's absolutely unobtainable unless you make some significant changes to the way you think about competition and the business you're in. These changes should not be mistaken for ideas on rebranding or incremental value changes but a way of thinking that surprises the market again and again with exciting, unexpected solutions. A way of thinking that produces an unconventional strategy that leaves competitors scrambling to catch up. A way of thinking that turns consumer expectations upside down and takes an industry into its next generation. It is called disruptive thinking (Williams, 2011).

*disruptionllc.com*

**TURNKEY EBOOKS**

According to John Hagel, the co-chair of the Deloitte Center for the Edge, we have entered an age of continual disruption, which can be manifested in any of three different ways by which a new business approach can disrupt an incumbent leader: first, by rendering obsolete a significant part of an incumbent's existing assets or installed resource base; second, by requiring an incumbent to significantly cannibalize its existing revenue or profit stream to respond to the new approach; or, third, by offering a new set of assumptions regarding the drivers of value creation and capture relative to the assumptions that have been the basis for the success of current incumbents. What makes disruptions so disruptive is that they "turn the assets of incumbents into potentially life threatening liabilities."

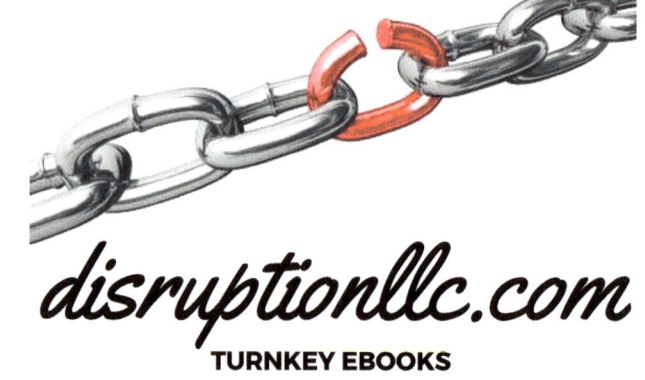

disruptionllc.com

**TURNKEY EBOOKS**

In all three instances, reacting effectively to a disruption can be challenging because it "requires incumbents to radically change their view of the world and embark on a very painful transition that will significantly erode performance in the short-term"3—a prospect that can be particularly problematic for publicly traded companies that feel compelled to keep investors happy on a quarter-to-quarter basis. In fact, Hagel noted, incumbents have an "almost infinite" capacity to rationalize why responding to disruptive challenges is not necessary. Conventional wisdom holds that, in the absence of equilibrium, adaptation is the best strategy. According to this view, executives will succeed if they can sense and respond quickly to what's changing around them. However, as important as adaptation is, it misses the real opportunity. Consider these examples, widely separated by time and by market: Malcolm McLean's efforts to evangelize containerized shipping in the 1950s and 1960s; Visa's redefinition of the credit card business in the 1970s (now called the "payments business");

Microsoft and Intel's turbocharging of the personal computer marketplace in the early 1980s; Li & Fung's new approaches to supply chain orchestration in the apparel industry in the 1980s and 1990s; and more recent influences by Google on the advertising business, by Facebook on social networking, and by Salesforce.com on enterprise software. In each case, the company aspired to do something far bolder than simply shape the performance of its own enterprises—it strove to shape global ecosystems and thereby fundamentally alter industries and markets (Hagel III, Brown, & Davison, 2008). This is what disruptive thinking requires, a marked paradigm shift that will lead to major upheaval in the way things are done. Disruption is sometimes erroneously exchanged for innovation. This is erroneous in the sense that these two terms are distinct except for sharing a characteristic of ingenuity. Disruptors are innovators, but not all innovators are disruptors in the same way that a square is a rectangle but not all rectangles are squares. Innovation and disruption are similar in that they are both makers and builders. Disruption takes a left turn by literally uprooting and changing how we think, behave, do business, learn and go about our day to day (Howard, 2013).

**TURNKEY EBOOKS**

Author of the investor's dilemma, Clayton Christensen says that a disruption displaces an existing market, industry, or technology and produces something new and more efficient and worthwhile. It is at once destructive and creative. Christensen fused these too often mixed terms, innovation and disruption to form a compound word "disruption innovation," which refers to the idea that an innovation transforms an existing market or sector by introducing simplicity, convenience, accessibility and affordability where complication and high cost are the status quo. This new idea, way of doing business, product or service then redefines the sector (Elsey, 2015). The concept of disruption innovation is exemplified in the rise of Android in the smartphone market, which was to the detriment of heavyweights such as Nokia and Blackberry. These two companies held the attention of all smartphone consumers; however, the simplicity, convenience, affordability, and versatility of Android Operating system and Android devices in general, caused a disruptive change of focus in consumers.

*disruptionllc.com*
**TURNKEY EBOOKS**

Clayton Christiansen is today's predominant voice on disruptive innovation. Disruptive innovation, a term of art coined by Christensen, describes a process by which a product or service takes root initially in simple applications at the very bottom of a market and then relentlessly moves up market, eventually displacing established competitors' systems. See below some key conceptual information taken from his website.

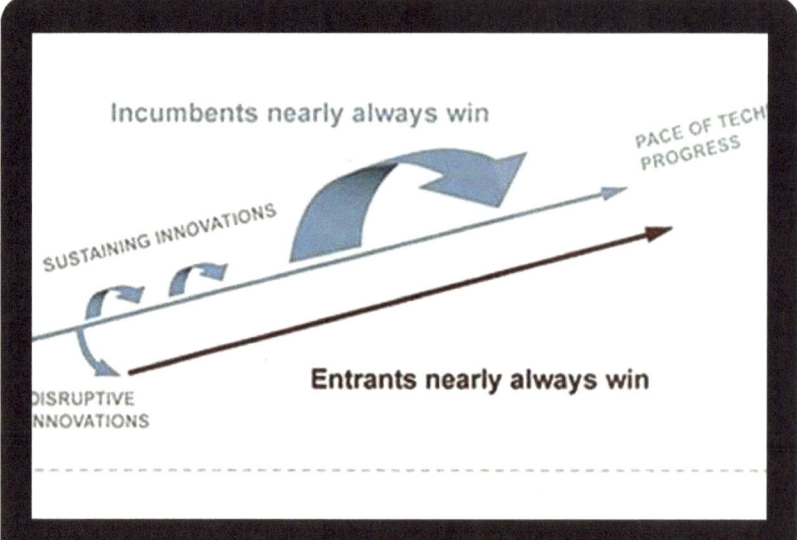

**TURNKEY EBOOKS**

As companies tend to innovate faster than their customers' needs evolve, most organizations eventually end up producing products or services that are actually too sophisticated, too expensive, and too complicated for many customers in their market. Companies pursue these "sustaining innovations" at the higher tiers of their markets because this is what has historically helped them succeed: by charging the highest prices to their most demanding and sophisticated customers at the top of the market, companies will achieve the greatest profitability.

However, by doing so, companies unwittingly open the door to "disruptive innovations" at the bottom of the market. An innovation that is disruptive allows a whole new population of consumers at the bottom of a market access to a product or service that was historically only accessible to consumers with a lot of money or a lot of skill.

TURNKEY EBOOKS

Characteristics of disruptive businesses, at least in their initial stages, can include: lower gross margins, smaller target markets, and simpler products and services that may not appear as attractive as existing solutions when compared against traditional performance metrics. Because these lower tiers of the market offer lower gross margins, they are unattractive to other firms moving upward in the market, creating space at the bottom of the market for new disruptive competitors to emerge.

# disruptionllc.com
**TURNKEY EBOOKS**

**Nikola Tesla was a Serbian American inventor, electrical engineer, mechanical engineer, physicist, and futurist best known for his contributions to the design of the modern alternating current electricity supply system. Tesla is the father of modern electricity. He helped disrupt the salt industry. Tesla was born: July 10, 1856, Smiljan, Croatia & Died: January 7, 1943, Manhattan, NY Significant designs: Induction motor, Tesla coil**

"The scientists of today think deeply instead of clearly. One must be sane to think clearly, but one can think deeply and be quite insane." "Our virtues and our failings are inseparable, like force and matter. When they separate, man is no more." "The present is theirs; the future, for which I really worked, is mine."

**TURNKEY EBOOKS**

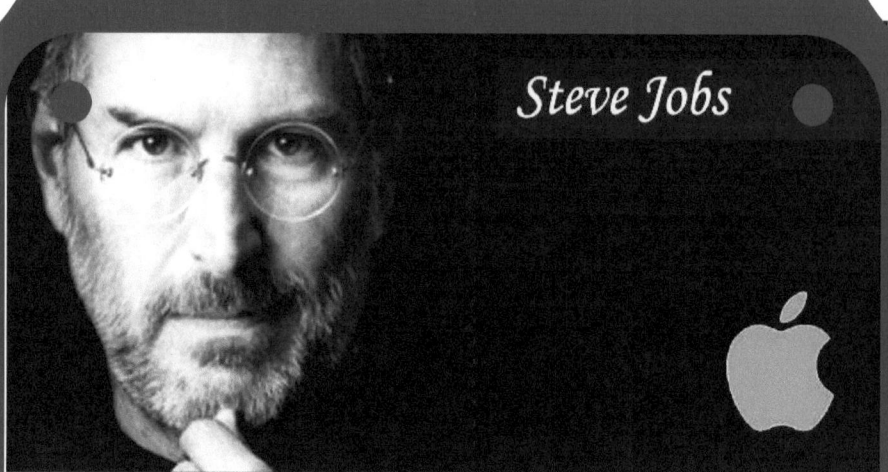

# Steve Jobs

Steven Paul "Steve" Jobs born February 24, 1955 and passed away October 5, 2011. Jobs was an American information technology entrepreneur and inventor. He was the co-founder, chairman, and chief executive officer (CEO) of Apple Inc.; CEO and largest shareholder of Pixar Animation Studios; a member of The Walt Disney Company's board of directors following its acquisition of Pixar; and founder, chairman, and CEO of NeXT Inc. Jobs is widely recognized as a pioneer of the microcomputer revolution of the 1970s, along with Apple co-founder Steve Wozniak. Shortly after his death, Jobs's official biographer, Walter Isaacson, described him as a "creative entrepreneur whose passion for perfection and ferocious drive revolutionized six industries: personal computers, animated movies, music, phones, tablet computing, and digital publishing."

*disruptionllc.com*

**TURNKEY EBOOKS**

Jobs's countercultural lifestyle and philosophy was a product of the time and place of his upbringing. Jobs was adopted at birth in San Francisco and raised in a hotbed of counterculture, the San Francisco Bay Area during the 1960s. As a senior at Homestead High in Cupertino, California, his two closest friends were the older engineering student (and Homestead High alumnus) Wozniak and his girlfriend, the artistically inclined and countercultural Homestead High junior Chrisann Brennan. Jobs and Wozniak bonded over their mutual fascination with Jobs's musical idol Bob Dylan, discussing his lyrics and collecting bootleg reel-to-reel tapes of Dylan's concerts. Jobs later dated Joan Baez who notably had a prior relationship with Dylan. Jobs briefly attended Reed College in 1972 before dropping out. He then decided to travel through India in 1974 and to study Zen Buddhism. Jobs's declassified FBI report says an acquaintance knew that Jobs used illegal drugs in college including marijuana.

**TURNKEY EBOOKS**

# VAYNERMEDIA

Vaynerchuk immigrated to the U.S. in 1978, and moved with his family to Edison, New Jersey. After graduating from Mount Ida College in Newton, MA, he transformed his father's Springfield, New Jersey liquor store into a retail wine store named Wine Library, and in 2006 started the video blog Wine Library TV, a daily internet webcast on the subject of wine and played a role in disrupting traditional marketing.

In 2011, Vaynerchuk announced he would step away from his daily wine video series to focus his attention on VaynerMedia, the social media brand consulting agency he co-founded in the spring of 2009. Vaynerchuk describes social media as a cocktail party, where brands must be a part of conversations that people have.

**TURNKEY EBOOKS**

## Wine Library

After graduating from college in 1998, Vaynerchuk assumed day to day control of his father's liquor store, then called Shopper's Discount Liquors. Through a combination of ecommerce, email marketing, and aggressive pricing, Vaynerchuk grew the business from $3 million to $50 million a year by 2005.
In 2009, Gary, along with his brother AJ Vaynerchuk, founded VaynerMedia, a social media-focused digital agency. The company focuses on providing social media and strategy services to Fortune 500 companies such as General Electric, Anheuser-Busch, Mondelez, and PepsiCo. In 2015, VaynerMedia was named one of AdAge's A-List agencies.

**TURNKEY EBOOKS**

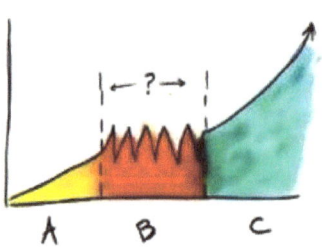

Aaron Ross is author of Predictable Revenue: Turn Your Business into a Sales Machine with the $100 Million Best Practices of Salesforce.com. GROW REVENUE BY 300% OR MORE AND MAKE IT PREDICTABLE... Aaron's system is built for disruptive companies.

"Alexander Graham Bell discovered the telephone, Thomas Edison discovered electricity and Aaron Ross discovered the Enterprise Market for Salesforce.com."

**TURNKEY EBOOKS**

Mark Elliot Zuckerberg born May 14, 1984 is an American computer programmer, Internet entrepreneur, and philanthropist. He is the chairman, chief executive, and co-founder of the social networking website Facebook. His net worth is estimated to be $48.2 billion as of 2016, and he is the face of the disruptive millennial entrepreneur.

**TURNKEY EBOOKS**

With his college roommates and fellow Harvard University students Eduardo Saverin, Andrew McCollum, Dustin Moskovitz, and Chris Hughes, Zuckerberg launched Facebook from Harvard's dormitory rooms. The group then introduced Facebook to other campuses. Facebook expanded rapidly, with one billion users by 2012. Zuckerberg was involved in various legal disputes that were initiated by others in the group, who claimed a share of the company based upon their involvement during the development phase of Facebook. Check out "The Social Network" movie and enjoy the story.

In December 2012, Zuckerberg and his wife Priscilla Chan announced they would give the majority of their wealth over the course of their lives to "advancing human potential and promoting equality" in the spirit of The Giving Pledge. On December 1, 2015, they announced they would give 99% of their Facebook shares (worth about $45 billion at the time) to the Chan Zuckerberg Initiative.

TURNKEY EBOOKS

Michael E. "Mike" Reynolds is an American architect based in New Mexico, known for the design and construction of "Earthship" passive solar homes. He is a proponent of "radically sustainable living". He has been a critic of the profession of architecture for reusing unconventional building materials from waste streams, such as automobile tires, and is known for designs that test the limits of building codes in a truly disruptive way.

*disruptionllc.com*

**TURNKEY EBOOKS**

Earthships can be built in any part of the world and still provide electricity, potable water, contained sewage treatment and sustainable food production. The most versatile and economical sustainable green building design in the world is an Earthship.

*disruptionllc.com*

**TURNKEY EBOOKS**

Peddle your bike for an hour and power your home for 24 hours. Fitness centers become mini power plants and homeowners own power capabilities. Cost around $200.

## disruptionllc.com
**TURNKEY EBOOKS**

Manoj Bhargava is an Indian American businessman, philanthropist, and visionary entrepreneur. He is the founder and CEO of Innovations Ventures LLC (dba Living Essentials LLC); the company is known for producing the 5 hour Energy drink. By 2012 the brand had grown to do an estimated $1 billion in sales. In 2015, Bhargava pledged 99% of his net worth to improving the wellbeing of the worlds less fortunate. Bhargava is also CEO of Stage 2 Innovations and inventor of the FREE electric bike that will change the way electricity is distributed globally.

**TURNKEY EBOOKS**

Elon Reeve Musk was born June 28, 1971 is a South Africanborn Canadian-American business tycoon, engineer, inventor and investor. He is the founder, CEO and CTO of SpaceX; co-founder, CEO and product architect of Tesla Motors; chairman of SolarCity, co-chairman of OpenAI; co-founder of Zip2; and co-founder of PayPal.

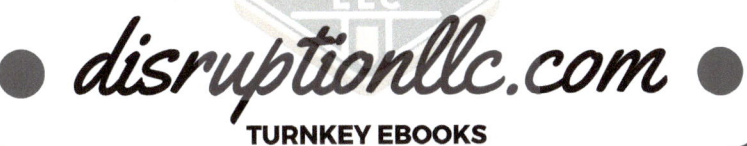

**TURNKEY EBOOKS**

As of April 2016, he has an estimated net worth of US$14.2 billion, making him one of the wealthiest individuals in the US. Musk has stated that the goals of SolarCity, Tesla Motors, and SpaceX revolve around his vision to change the world and humanity. His goals include reducing global warming through sustainable energy production and consumption, and reducing the "risk of human extinction" by "making life multi-planetary" by establishing a human colony on Mars. He has envisioned a high-speed transportation system known as the Hyperloop, and has proposed a VTOL supersonic jet aircraft with electric fan propulsion, known as the Musk electric jet.

## References

Adler, R., & Firestone, C. M. (2015). Navigating Continual Disruption.

Desjardins, J. (2014, July 9). How Bitcoin can and will disrupt the financial system. Retrieved April 5, 2016, form http://www.visualcapitalist.com/how-bitcoin-can-and-will-disrupt-financial-system/

Elsey, W. (2015, April 28). Is There Disruption In The Philanthropic Sector?. Retrieved April 5, 2016, from http://ezinearticles.com/?Is-¬There-¬Disruption-¬In-¬The-¬Philanthropic-¬Sector?&id=9012794

Elsey, W. (2015, April 21). What are Disruption and Innovation? Retrieved April 5, 2016, from http://ezinearticles.com/?What-¬Are-¬Disruption-¬and-¬Innovation?&id=9004454

Hagel, J., Brown, J. S., & Davison, L. (2008). Shaping strategy in a world of constant disruption. Harvard Business Review, 86(10), 80-89.

Howard, C. (2013, March 27). Disruption Vs. Innovation: What's The Difference? Retrieved April 5, 2016, from http://www.forbes.com/sites/carolinehoward/2013/03/27/you-say-innovator-i-say-disruptor-whats-the-difference/#62beacadbd79

Roose, K. (2014, June 1). Is Silicon Valley the Future of Finance? Retrieved April 5, 2016, from http://nymag.com/daily/intelligencer/2014/05/is-silicon-valley-the-future-of-finance.html

Saitto, S. (2014, December 4). Uber Valued at $40 Billion in $1.2 Billion Equity Funding. Retrieved April 5, 2016, from http://www.bloomberg.com/news/articles/2014-12-04/uber-valued-at-40-billion-with-1-2-billion-equity-fundraising

TURNKEY EBOOKS

Utterback, J. M., & Acee, H. J. (2003, November). Disruptive technology. In Keith Pavitt Conference, University of Sussex, UK (Vol. 14).

Wang, R. (2014, December 19). Cloud is the 'Foundation for Digital Transformation. Retrieved April 5, 2016, from http://www.forbes.com/sites/oracle/2014/12/19/ray-wang-cloud-is-the-foundation-for-digital-transformation/#6a84177417e1

Williams, L. (2011). Disruptive Thinking: The Revolution Is in Full Swing. Pearson Education, Inc.

## Thanks for reading
## Please Reveiw

### disruptionllc.com
**TURNKEY EBOOKS**

Disruption is a perennial factor in every human endeavor and it behooves every company to accommodate, or cause disruption or be disrupted.

Be the change. Make an impact.
Take a big risk.

Joyfully disrupt the natural order of things.

Adam White, CEO
Disruption, LLC

**TURNKEY EBOOKS**

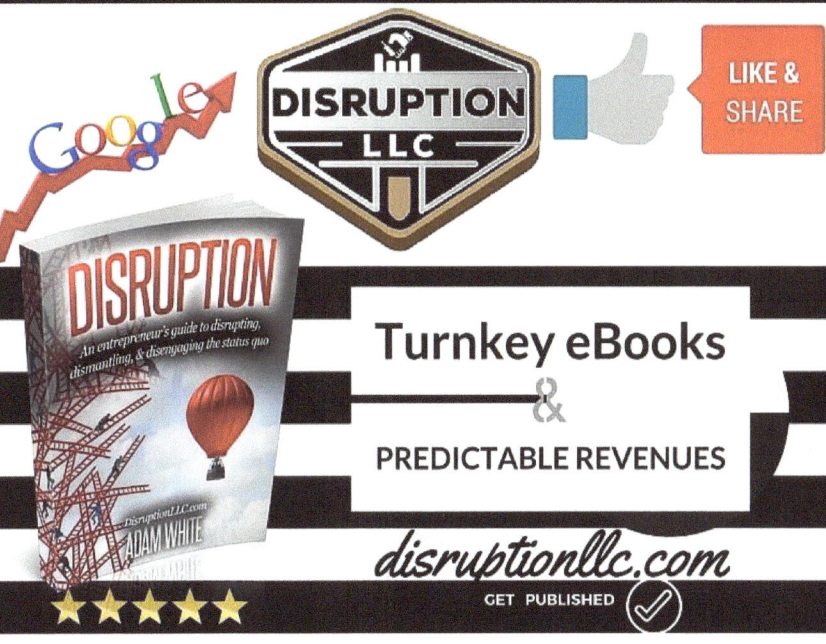

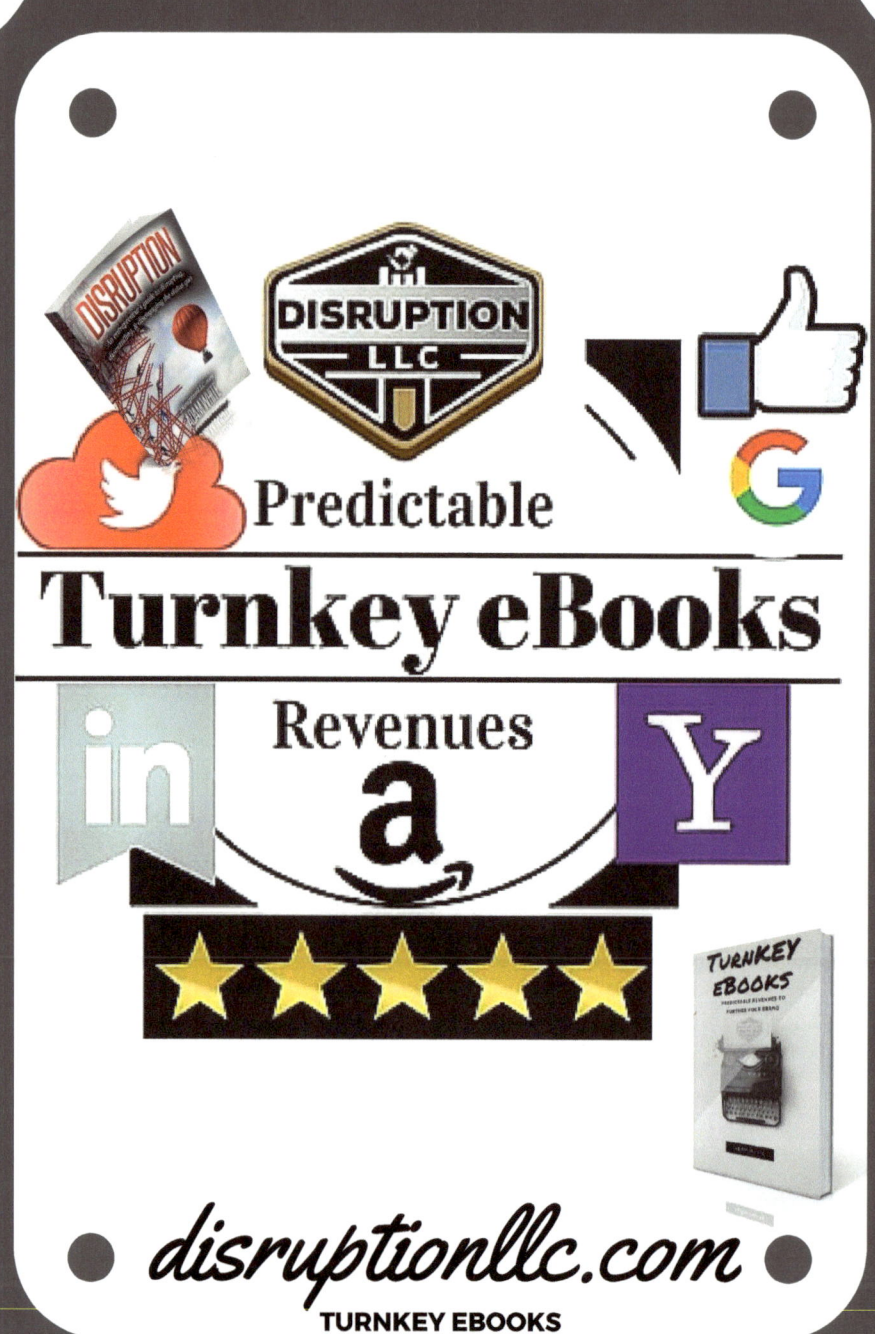

 # Turnkey eBooks
## & Predictable Revenues
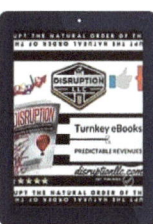

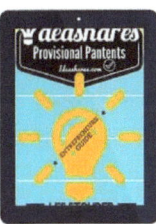  

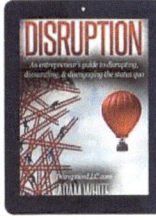      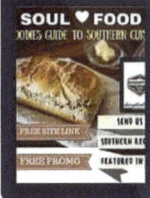

## disruptionllc.com
**TURNKEY EBOOKS**

# Earn Royalties
# Internationally

**Four easy installments of $500**

Earnest Agreement
Promo Video
Pre-Launch Publication
Final Publication

Generate sales & earn royalties prior to publishing with our pre launch publication.

# E-BOOK Publishing

# #amazonkindle

# Amazon Kindle
# Support & Service

**90 DAY** — **E-book Publishing**

**Are you an expert on a topic?**
- Be Internationally Published
- Earn Predictable Revenues
- Gain Lifetime Royalties

*Soup to nuts service. Satisfaction guaranteed.*

Lebanon, TN USA

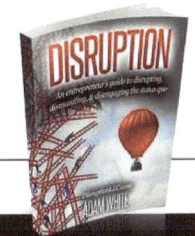

# #ebookpro

# E-BOOK PUBLISHING

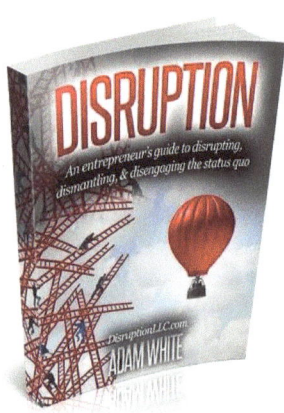

Amazon Kindle Services & Support

International Royalties

Generate Predictable Revenues

**Disruption**
Main: (615) 715 7408

# #TOPSTARTUP

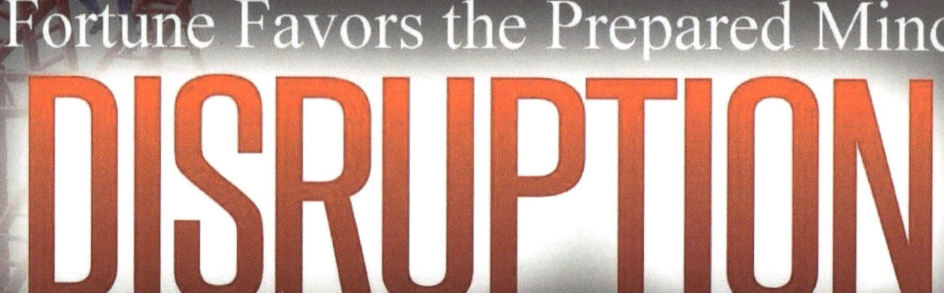

# Fortune Favors the Prepared Mind
# DISRUPTION

*An entrepreneur's guide to disrupting, dismantling, & disengaging the status quo*

Fostering Entrepreneurship & Effecting Change

DisruptionLLC.com

# ADAM WHITE

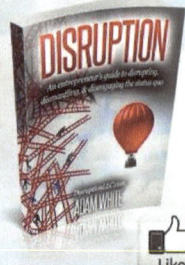

★★★★★